洞月亮

CAVE MOON PRESS
YAKIMA 中 WASHINGTON

2016

Footsteps:
Poems for Homeless Veterans

Edited by

Paul Nelson and Doug Johnson

月亮
CAVE MOON PRESS
YAKIMA 中 WASHINGTON

© Copyright 2016 Reserved by each contributing poet. All work is used with permission by Cave Moon Press
All rights reserved.
Artwork by: Alfredo Arreguin- used with permission
Book Design: Doug Johnson

ISBN: 978-0692747100

Footsteps:

Poems for Homeless Veterans

Acknowledgments

Thank you to Alfredo Arreguin for allowing us to use *Tierra y Libertad (Homage to Emiliano Zapata)* 60" x 48", 2003 for the cover.

Thank you to Liu Xiangxia for Mandarin translation help on the cover, as well.

"I Have Never Wanted to March" Previously published in *Dear Ghoss* Graywolf Press, 2006.

"The Sister Next to be Born" Previously published in *Furies: A Poetry Anthology of Women Warriors.*

"Gunner Apoligizes for Not Shooting" Previously published in *Hawaii Pacific Review.* Hawai'i Pacific U. Vol. 19. Honolulu, HI. 2005; *Pontoon 8.* Floating Bridge Press. Seattle, WA. Number 8. 2005; *Meridian Anthology Of Contemporary Poetry.* #4. Cyprian Publishers. Naples, FL. 2006.

"Gunner Tells What Happened" Previously published in *Carquinez Poetry Review.* Small Poetry Press. Crockett, CA. #3. 2005.

"American Sentences Blogged When My Son-in-law Served in Iraq" Previously published by *San Diego City Works Press.*

"Castle Rock" Previously published in *Flesh Becomes Word*, Dos Madres Press, 2013.

"Herb Parker Feels Like Dancing" previously published in *Plume*, University of Washington Press. Seattle, 2012.

"Inner Feelings," "The Boat," and "Miracle" Previously published in Green Cammie, Floating Bridge Press, 2010.

Thank you to Deborah Woodard, representing Crysta Casey's Estate, for allowing us to use Crysta's work.

Foreword

I was leafing through the galley of this book and came to *Today The Deer* by Charles Potts. I met Charles a couple of decades ago first through Red Sky Poetry Theater, but in the context of this book you are holding, a poem of his I published in a different anthology also comes to mind. It is:

> *The Task Master*
>
> Your job
> Makes no difference
> Whether or not you accept it
> Avoid getting hit by falling pieces of the empire

It's classic, sardonic, Potts and it's funny until you realize that the pieces of crumbling empire fall first on those less fortunate, those at the margins. The stats on the back cover remind us that 11% of homeless in the U.S. are veterans and 50% are age 51 or older. The fall of the empire has begun and there is nothing funny about the way veterans are treated. People of conscience have to step up and, despite how they might feel about the incredibly awful priorities of the U.S. empire, the 1,000 military bases, drones, gulags, torture, treatment of those who carry out the endless violent occupations of our day, despite all this, we must have compassion for those who bought the propaganda that there is honor in all this. Veterans are the second casualties of the empire's crash, shortly after the truth, which is always the first casualty of war or empire.

And if any poem does its work, it allows us a moment outside of time, a moment of transcendence. It allows us to see something familiar in a new way, or to see something we've always felt or intuited to be expressed quite clearly in words or images. There is so much poetry here that does that, some with a direct connection to the themes of veterans and war, or the traces left by people who are no longer here, their footsteps, some not so directly.

It was an honor to participate in one of Doug Johnson's elegant anthologies and I hope this does something to assuage the pain and suffering of homeless veterans.

peN
6pm - 7.20.16

Introduction

To celebrate ten years of helping communities Cave Moon Press has produced this book to aid homeless veterans. This is a book of witness to the invisible. Cave Moon Press is blessed to be a part of such a rich artistic community.

Soldiers march for liberty.
Carbon footprints stomp watersheds.
People wander without hope.

As a poet holds their duty to the page, soldiers hold their duty to serve. Others hold their duty to the environment. We all know of someone setting out on their quest without ever getting the homecoming of Odysseus. When duties disillusion people wander.

This book is to honor the people instead of the causes. Cars wage war on the environment. Politics change like the newspaper wrapping fish. The invisible still wander. Write to honor the ignored. After publication it is hoped that each accepted poet will combine readings around food and music with proceeds going to the local homeless network of their choice.

This can be through your VA or YMCA programs. In Seattle we will be contributing to Facing Homelessness, but feel free to find your own way to bring awareness and resources to homeless veterans in your area. Feel free to contact us with questions.

Take Care.
Doug Johnson

This is dedicated to all who wander

Table of Contents

Charles O'Hay
Perchance to Dream..1
A Walk in the Forest of Milk..2
Pilgrimage..3

Tess Gallagher
I Have Never Wanted to March..5

Jerome Gold
Everything that Fell...9
Icarus..10

Doug Johnson
Hey, Diddle, Diddle, Left, Left, Left..12

Kathleen Flenniken
Herb Parker Feels Like Dancing...13

Gerry McFarland
Gunner Apologizes for Not Shooting......................................16
Gunner Tells What Happened..17

Charles Potts
Today the Deer..18

Michael Daley
War Crimes...19

Sam Hamill
Children of the Marketplace...21

Paul Nelson
82. Automedicador (For Amalio)..23
90. Slow Down Tahoe Driver..25

Amalio Madueño
Garcia Walks..27
Garcia Crosses the Border...29

Jenifer Browne Lawrence
The Sister Next to be Born..31

Denise Calvetti Michaels
American Sentences Blogged When my Son-In-Law
Served in Iraq...32
Jack Remick
Daesh Kills the Bearded Bulls...34
T. Clear
While You Wander...36
Abide..38
Thomas Hubbard
Ahh, Tootsie, Is that You?..39
Lawrence Matsuda
Homecoming...40
Five Steps—Five By Seven..42
Nisei Fall..43
Angelee Deodhar
Cradle Board..44
José Kozer
Chanoyú...45
Chanoyú (Translation by **Judith K. LangHilgartner**)..............51
Cántico Espiritual...56
Spiritual Canticle (Translation by **Judith K. Lang Hilgartner**)........61
Liz Dolan
That Summer...65
After Hiroshima..66
Emmanuel Williams
Front Line Man...67
Jason Kirk
Untitled Haiku...68
Untitled Haiku...69
Brian Volck
Castle Rock..70

Kristine Iredale
Dropping the Ball..73
David Pointer
Main Street Banishment...74
Destierro de Avenida Central..75
Manila John Basilone...76
Manila John Basilone (Español)...77
Clinical Pearl Incinerator...78
Incinerador de Perla Clínico..79
Crysta E. Casey
Inner Feelings..80
The Boat...81
Miracle..83
V.A. Smoke Shack..84

Perchance to Dream

All over, people are asleep. Night sleep.
Mid-afternoon naps. Sleep after sex.
Sleep in bus station chairs. Hungover sleep.

Some are dreaming of death
the way prisoners dream of tunnels.
Some are dreaming of tomorrow
as though it were a country on a map
they can't unfold.

Some simply dream
long strings of letters like paper dolls
across the windows of their minds.

As if waiting for someone they love
to come home. Someone who's been away
a long time. Someone who'll pause
before the inevitable embrace
to take it all in.

Some will awake to kisses. Some
to the smell of dinner adrift on the lake of air
that laps at the sheets.

Others will wake to a boot. Or
to footsteps in the hall. Footsteps
owned by a man who wants the rent.
A fist bolted to the arm he uses
to knock his roomers awake.

—*Charles O'Hay*

A Walk in the Forest of Milk

I pull a snow apple from a tree,
take a bite, and feel the flesh
become words in my mouth.

Anything that flowers here
does so in secret,
the way a new thought has only itself
for company.

The stream moves as a train
from one abandoned town to another,
adding nothing, leaving nothing
behind.

How many times
have I written you this letter
only to tear it up?
And begin again.

—Charles O'Hay

Pilgrimage

Wearing the magnolia kasaya
and sandals of their faith
the young Buddhist monks walk
to the corner bodega for smokes.

Like schoolboys
about to enter a liquor store
they travel in groups
speaking quietly among themselves.

Inside I stand in line behind
a monk with beefy ears
as he asks the clerk
whether he sells lottery tickets.

The clerk nods yes
and the monk recites the numbers
his voice soft
as kneaded cloth.

When he is done, he pays
for his tickets and leaves.
I step up to the glass and say,
"Give me the numbers he played."

The clerk smiles, punches in
the numbers, and hands me my tickets.
"Namaste," I tell him, bow,
and walk out.

The next day at the store I check
the board. Not a winner
in the boatload. Another lesson
in non-attachment.

—Charles O'Hay

I Have Never Wanted to March

or wear an epaulet. Once I walked
in a hometown parade to celebrate
a salmon derby. I was seven, my hair in
pigtails, a steel flasher strapped diagonally
across my chest *bandolier*-style
(in Catalan *bandolera* from *banda*—band
of people–and *bandoler* meaning bandit).
My black bandit boots were rubber
because here on the flanks of the Olympics
it always rains on our parades.

I believe I pushed a doll buggy.
I believe all parades, especially military
parades, could be improved if
the soldiers wore *bandoliers* made to attract
fish, and if each soldier pushed a doll buggy
inside which were real-seeming babies,
their all-seeing doll-eyes open
to reflect the flight of birds, of balloons
escaped from the hands of children to
hover over the town—higher than flags, higher
than minarets and steeples.

What soldier could forget
collateral damage with those baby faces
locked to their chin straps? It is
conceivable soldiers would resist
pushing doll buggies. Bending over
might spoil the rigidity of their marching.
What about a manual exhorting the patriotic

duty of pushing doll buggies? Treatises
on the symbolic meaning would need to be
written. Hollywood writers might be of use.
Poets and historians could collaborate,
reminding the marchers of chariots, of
Trojan horses, of rickshaws, of any wheeled
conveyance ever pulled, pushed or driven
in the service of humankind.

I would like, for instance, to appear
in the next parade as a Trojan horse. When
they open me I'll be seven years old.
There will be at least seven of me
inside me, for effect, and because it's
a mystical number. I won't understand
much about war, in any case—especially
its good reasons. I'll just want to be pushed
over some border into enemy territory, and
when no one's thinking anything except: what
a pretty horse! I'll throw open myself
like a flank and climb out, all
seven of me, like a many-legged spider
of myself. I'll speak only
in poetry, my second language, because it
is beautifully made for exploring the miraculous
ordinary event—in which an alchemy
of words agrees to apprentice itself to the possible
as it evades the impossible. Also poetry
doesn't pretend to know answers and speaks best
in questions, the way children do
who want to know everything, and don't believe
only what they're told. I'll be seven

unruly children when they open me up,
and I'll invite the children of the appointed enemy
to climb into my horse for a ride. We'll be secret
together, the way words are
the moment before they are spoken—
those Trojan horses of silence, looking for a border

to roll across like oversized toys
manned by serious children—until one horse
has been pushed back and forth
with its contraband of mutually pirated children
so many times it will be clear to any adult watching
this unseemly display, that enemy territory
is everywhere when anyone's child is at stake, when
the language of governments is reduced to ultimatums,
when it wants to wear epaulets
and to march without
its doll buggy.

But maybe and edict or two could be made
by one child-ventriloquist through the mouth
of the horse, proposing that the advent of atrocities
be forestalled by much snorting, neighing, prancing and
tail swishing—by long, exhausted parades
of reciprocal child-hostages who may be
rescued only in the language of poetry
which insists on being lucid
and mysterious at once, like a child's hand
appearing from under the tail
of the horse, blindly waiving to make sure that anyone
lined up along the street does not submit entirely
to the illusion of their absence, their

ever-squandered innocence, their hyper-responsive
minds in which a ladybug would actually fly away,
with only its tiny flammable wings,
to save its children from the burning house.

—*Tess Gallagher*

Everything That Fell

We mowed down the forest with bulldozers,
cleared the red soil of everything that grew.
All that soft wood, all those porous stalks,
those ropey vines and spiked leaves—
In two months, we burned everything that fell
and that was everything.

One day in the middle of this a man
running from fire of a different kind came
out of the shade of the remaining trees.
He wore the classic black pajamas
and an expression of bewilderment.
He ran back into the forest, and out again.
The place where he could hide was gone.
The place to which he had adapted his life, focused
his memories—gone. What must he have thought?
Had his wife given birth here (there had been a village)?
Had he met here with others to plan an ambush?
Did he call out the names of his parents, his brothers?
You might say his death was a result of his
failure to adapt to a changed environment.
In those days we had all gone feral.

—Jerome Gold

Icarus

for Roy McCready

From the ground I might have seemed
an angel falling out of orbit
or a tiny meteor aflame
spinning on it lopsided axis
arc-ing downward to a terrible rendezvous.

Inside, beginning to burn, I sat,
unable to reach an ejection handle,
anticipating the melt and crackle of my eyeballs.
My brain, working at light's speed,
fastened finally on the solution to my problem:

I would ride the plane into the sea,
the sea would douse the fire,
I would climb out and be saved.
I held to this desperate idiocy for an
electric moment's fraction before my plane exploded,

loosing me into hot sunlight
where my parachute snapped, rippled,
opened and set me down in brine
that doused my burns. The helicopter
arrived before the enemy and I was saved,

though somewhere in the tangle of shouting and harness,
drumming rotor blades and lathering water,
and the fearful hammering of cannon
I lost my Navy-issue .38-caliber
revolver

which
as I healed in hospital in San Diego,
the FBI, in a confrontation classic in irony,
dispassion, and the agency's determination
to extinguish evil in all its guises,

accused me of stealing with the motive of
profit, or nostalgia, or
providing aid to the enemy.

—Jerome Gold

Hey Diddle, Left, Left, Left.

—For the Tabayoyon sons

You earned the Bronze Star. Left. Left. Left, Right Left.
To block the memories of body parts. Left. Left. Left, Right Left.
Tour after tour and a hey diddle, diddle
Tour after tour. Left. Left. Left, Right, Left.

Dad wanted to take you to dinner. Left. Left. Left.
I can't Dad. There's blood on my boots
Afghanistan to McCord AFB. Right.
You don't understand. I'm not your son

I'm not the same person. Left. Left. Right.
Three hundred miles to the V.A.
local clinics can't fill your meds,
Hey diddle, diddle, whiskey to wet your whistle. Left.

Still lost in the Afghani desert
Stumbling footsteps today and a hey diddle, diddle. Right.

—Doug Johnson

Herb Parker Feels Like Dancing

—Richland, 1949

Mr. Parker's Sunbeam is shiny as an atom.
He pulls up, alights with grace
and makes his dance hall entrance.
Perhaps you sense his English accent
and pocket square. Women shy
like ponies to one corner. He corrals one
and trots her around the dance floor.

Herb Parker rides a shapely 4/4.
"That Old Black Magic,"
"Baby, It's Cold Outside."
Maybe it is, or maybe it's blazing,
unsafe to breathe tonight.

Her earrings are zircon daisies.
A silver belt rings her slim waist.
Herb Parker steers her toward
his dark place. "Mr. Parker?"
he hears somebody ask, like a tremble
on a seismograph, but you can't blame
Herbert Parker for his appetites.

He palms the tender center of
her back. "Mr. Parker?" again.
Perhaps it's her voice, or her husband's,
or one of the voices in his head. He's

a Dutch master with his finger in the dike,
a valvular, crepuscular figure.

"Look out the window at that storm ..."
He takes the government's calls
and negotiates those devil's bargains,
how much of their order can he fill?
You understand they say "product"
and mean plutonium, they mean
how many bombs can you afford to fuel?
"Darling, down and down I go,

round and round I go in a spin" ...
the river, and its sediments,
the air, capricious with winds,
the soil column, the ground water,
the vase of wildflowers on Deputy Chief
Gamertsfelder's desk! Native species
sprouting in Richland yards.
The mosquitoes, for pity's sake,
the farm animals, the farmers living
off the land, the water birds and the
duck hunters, the bottom fish and
the fishermen on Richland dock.
Everything he thinks to test ... good god,

the entire food chain contaminated.
He's basically a shy man with
immeasurable power. A sultan
coaxing his courtesan's smile.
She only shakes a little now.
Don't you understand? Someone

must step forward and play God.
How much better that the man
can lead? hold you tight
in his very good hands, and spin.

—Kathleen Flenniken

GUNNER APOLOGIZES FOR NOT SHOOTING

Somewhere over the hot water lay the enemy.
Don't know what they're gonna do, Captain says,
our faces parallel at battle stations.
Sure, we're nuclear. But they're crazy.
Keep your butt up, boy.

The rivet of my helmet dug into my scalp.
Nothing anywhere but ocean.

The enemy is always invisible, Captain says.
Until it's time to shoot. Brace yourself like a tripod.

My flack jacket hung on me. The flacking
started eight inches below my shoulder.
Plenty of room for a small rocket
or a series of shells in a neat parabola
to find me and my bowl of a helmet.

The best defense is a good offense, Captain says.
Shoot first. Two facts, Captain says, in military life:
follow any lawful order; and all orders are lawful.
Watch the endless horizon endlessly. Breathe,
bend your knees, grip the gun as if you would fall
without it, the knuckle loose at the trigger. Wait
for the enemy. Hold your position for twenty-five years.

—Gerry McFarland

Gunner Tells What Happened

From below where the tanks
of heat boiled he surfaced charred
boots first drenched with his last
sweat, cheeks and forehead blistered

perfect circumferences, islands
of pink skin strafed by fire.
Tied in a metal stretcher still dressed
he stares off as if in thought

about to ask the time or tell
how he smelled his death and let go.
Bearing their damp shipmate forward
they navigate this new continent

on the dark deck of the
disabled ship adrift and blind
in the Gulf of Tonkin, running lights
the only stars. How awkwardly

they set the body down. Their hands
fail them. They return for the next
body, three more yet, failing
silently as young men do.

—Gerry McFarland

Today the Deer

Today the deer
Her black hooves in the creek at the water's edge
Regards me way above on the road running by
Could she have heard that I was singing
The song my wife and I had her sister sing
At our wedding
Which I also played at her funeral
Simon's "Bridge over Troubled Water."

Every day a deer is killed
On Mill Creek Road or Blue Creek Road
Nobody minds the 40 and then 35 MPH speed limit sign.
There are dead deer everywhere.

My wife was run over on a road not far from here.
I watch the deer crossing in front of me
At night, in the fog, in daylight, at dawn and dusk.
For miles up the creek
I carry the deer's regarding gaze.

—Charles Potts

War Crimes

> *"Society is like a stew. If you don't stir it up every once in a while then a layer of scum floats to the top."* —Edward Abbey

The Senator was protecting, like a she-bear,
that revered Dr. K., whose damned body,
well past ninety and rotting in his slippers,
shuffled into the Senate to advise a subcommittee
underwhelmed by chanting protesters —
a Greek tragedy, his body wheeled in
from a movie set—Dr. Strangelove.
The Chorus chanted names of countries
where Henry's legacy arose, where
countless human animals boiled in
or fled our poisons, our strafing,
boots we crept in to make them safe.
When they chanted the name, "Vietnam,"
the Senator cried out. Once I had assumed
he spoke with my own heart.
I lied to myself that he knew the city streets,
could have been my classmate,
might have walked the old neighborhood,
struggled with us, knew what work is.
I blinded myself to his history of privilege.
He'd been chained to a wall in the prison hut,
so why bow to this war criminal,
frail seer led to testify before Creon
while the Chorus in pink was ushered offstage?
They may have felt it savage, compassionless,
to hiss at the defender of détente, intervention,
hemisphere hegemony, and overthrow—once,
the brain of Nixon, our blood line to the Hapsburgs.

When the Senator spewed his regal curse,
no one spoke. Protestors had defiled his hall,
calm proceedings gave him meaning,
an imagined hurt to Henry was a breach.
But the Senator hurt me, ratted my trust.
Not by sicking his slick and frothing dogs
to slime the staircase, but he whipped me
with my own guilt, that beautiful
inward machine. Pop indoctrination
and other Media distractions halted, even
the Prisoner of War unmasked as drone
of the dictator class, outraged, was silenced
for the moment, and those clowns, the Chorus
whispered: "War Crime War Crime War Crime."
Picture her swept into the arms of the suited guard,
the Code Pink girl who rushes Henry
shaking like Voodoo her shiny handcuffs,
the nauseated wife behind Schultz
flanked by two daughters in a trance—
the girl shoved away, pumps above the wreckage
of Kissinger her scrawled sign: "Cambodia,"
the Senator cursing her, cursing all of us
dredges up from his own inmost filth:
"Get out of here, you low-life scum."

Children of the Marketplace

They come out of nowhere, the sad-eyed
pleading children of the streets, they come
bearing shoplifted socks, small notebooks,
pens, anything, even just a card that pleads
for change, a peso so they can eat.

From our lunch spot under the grand
acacia trees, we say, "No, gracias," wondering
if a coin encourages thievery or whether
any of them will ever learn to read.
Or we make a gift of some small change
when one rushes to open the door
of a cab we've flagged. "No, gracias,"
to the old woman selling wilting roses
on the street, wondering what life
has she whose children learned to pick
a pocket, to moan for some relief
in a world without regrets, a world of need.

We watch a pregnant girl drag her heavy cart
through busy traffic on the street,
sorting through the trash—salvaging
old cardboard, plastic bottles, a board,
a brick, old newsprint, almost anything
that ordinary trash provides. Her work
is hard, her face a mask of grief
the marketplace can't hide.

In Seattle's Pioneer Square, it's a wrinkled face
asking for a dollar for the newspaper
of the homeless, news of that other marketplace
where human life, degraded or self-abused,
comes cheap, and dignity and hope
are long forgotten dreams.

It's the same in Caracas, Mumbai,
New York City or Saigon. The world is one.
Who knows what's wrong or right,
whose coin will go for suicidal wine
and whose for mercy in a shelter for the night?
The young, the old, for them there is
no sense of time, no past remembered,
no thought of what tomorrow brings.
The marketplace is full of things.

—Sam Hamill

82. AUTOMEDICADOR (FOR AMALIO)

> *He had his fortune invested in sheets, but one day he was robbed by a platoon of ghosts.*
> Ramon Gomez de la Serna

Turn Back! What's an automedicador w/o his pocket insulin? What's Garcia doing in the forsythia why Garcia under the Chinese Witch Hazel bush or puzzled by the Arboretum's Camper Down Elm? Garcia on acid for a week, a month, a year melting the walls of his brain maybe or just turning doors of perception into bliss and windows.

The legends of Garcia grow (still after the elusive metaphor) down by the river where he got his free sandals where he watches his step aware of Corua by the Embudo where it stripes itself with the Big River. Garcia eyeing the waitresses, ordering tuna tataki or sending tulips to the Lady of the house always to ward off the confusion of all sentient beings' erroneous views, usually projection Garcia sings, part Yaqui, part Jung, part Chinese, eating Crispy Pimp with Jidi Majia in Xining.

Garcia stabs himself w/ another needle for the hit of a warm hormone & regulate his fat metabolism stabb'd smack dab the middle of the island of his Yaqui belly without even an ouch and more than a pinch of gratitude. Garcia an oxy for his hip, a smile in his eye under the full blossom'd Cascadia cherry

tree on that rare March day. Holy Garcia laughing
laughing his hoarse man ghost laugh w/ overgrown
ear hair.

        The ghosts'll come
   one day, but not to
     day. Today Garcia
            orders one more Dragon
                      roll.

1:12P - 4.1.13

—Paul Nelson

90. Slow Down Tahoe Driver

(For Brian Love)

Our only real property consists of our bones.
—Ramon Gomez de la Serna

A hard way for the orbit to expand, the car crash & instant death after Independence Day. Bones & a hat they'd rescue from the spot where Auburn Way North becomes Auburn Way South, a crawl from the Rainbow bar, hard way for one's orbit to expand. A spot on the parade route. How your baritone'd call out each float, each entry, each Good Ol' Day moving outhouse rolls west on Main in Slaughter right there during the season of the Ripe Plum Full Moon, slow enough to practice the religion of plum blossoms unaware here's where the Tahoe'd blow through the red & blow a hole in our lives in one last t-bone. & the sunset the night you died, I know, Doc, I know, maybe I apply something angelic to rays affix themselves to clouds over West Hill. Maybe it's me projecting a need to see you've crossed over safe to be reunited with your speed & the Supreme Barber in the sky will cut off that god-forsaken beard, pour you a Scotch and water, wait for a story about the crosseyed prize bull at the Puyallup Fair.

Ilalqo's where waters come together, each stream unique to itself surrenders to a larger current, becomes something more than they'd be alone, one of those

25

vortexes were local tribes'd stop & linger, so slow they'd be, so deliberate. & there you'd be dubbing old Art Pepper cds, maybe listening to The Trip, the prison tale of stories told behind bars so ride the imagination for a while, a respite from the cell. Bones, Doc. That's all we own anyway & yours, how much longer could they take you inhaling cigars or any more Scotch anyway? We'd have wished for one last goodbye.

   Slow Down Tahoe Driver.
    You never know whose brother's
     on the other side.

8:27A - 7.7.13

—Paul Nelson

Garcia Walks

I've been walking for a thousand miles
I walk and walk and walk
The schemes I've walked through
    mechanized agriculture
    nuclear missiles
    suffering Madonna
    November 22nd
    Government Protection
    Spinning black holes
    Cold fusion tubes
    Black Monday
    Liars Poker
    Chaos Theory
The War on Drugs
Same sidewalks same streets same dogs same schemes
Different cities different states different names
I'm walking through a curtain of schemes
Each fold each pleat a silky obstacle
Whenever I see a scheme I walk right into it
I cheerfully walk through schemes
    Scheme of full employment
    Scheme of the rotary engine
    Scheme of the 900 number
    Scheme of solar energy
    Scheme of wind power
Scheme of total connection
Impressive such simple schemes
I love walking through them steaming greening misting darkening
What could happen to me as long as I keep walking

      Walk away from it all
      Walk into everything at once
      Walk with an angel bustle
      Walk for health and fitness
      Walk into a hall of mirrors for a course correction
      Walk away from myself
Is it someone (No! It's me!)
Walking into another scheme
If I stop walking will it be time to figure
Which was the most impressive?

Oh shut up and keep walking

—*Amalio Madueño*

Garcia Crosses the Border

Whenever he sleeps his mind is the north
Whenever he wakes the sun is going down
The moon is going down
Day after day the suburbs tilt away
Beyond the cars and sprinklers spraying
Preciously all the lawns and all the sidewalks
All the sound and all the money and hard hearts
And ruthless plans stretched for miles
Into Mojave traffic smog & smoke & soot

Everyone has been here before him
All their lies run hard ahead of him
Run into oncoming headlights
Run away down the grade
Where the city spreads out smoldering

He has more dreams than anyone
They rush out of him
Flying to the end of the road & pinned there
Against barbed wire chain link & oleander
Where each becomes a ghost of itself
      Ghost of well-being
      Ghost of wealth
      Ghost of home
      Ghost of the barrio
      Ghost of *la familia*
Walking the street he feels strong in his stride
As expectation tilts the day down the commercial strip
To the car lot and the bank and the fountains falling
Through the hours without desire without agents

He's one step ahead
He's the one who will never go back
He is the son lost forever in the crowd
He is the first he is the only

—*Amalio Madueño*

The Sister Next to Be Born

Isn't she the one who's prone to falling
from the clothesline, strand of hair sucked
to sable brush tip between her teeth?
The one we tracked from Little Chief smoker
to roadside shoulder pocketing coins of highway
drunks who palmed her sockeyes on the slope
below the snow, river long past melt, the sky strung
with milky lies we told at night — in our folded hands
the stolen smoke, kitchen match a siren call
across her zipper, flame like sunlight and the cheap
inhale out the door while father slept between
Zane Grey and Rainier. We woke him once to view
a purple ridge along her cheekbone. In drying time
the clothespin tries to mind her fish-quick tongue.

—*Jenifer Browne Lawrence*

American Sentences Blogged When My Son-In-Law Served in Iraq

One month after Michael leaves, red camellia buds in the window.

My daughter calls, embassy in green zone hit, everyone in lockdown.

Abe, an old friend with Alzheimer's said to Bush on TV, How dare you?

We break bread, last night's dinner an act of resistance, an act toward peace.

What is important but the need to wipe the counter, gather the crumbs?

Wolfer, killed in green zone, knew my son-in-law, both married with daughters.

I remember camping beneath the stars in the nave between the trees.

We were a family, our tent pitched on the precipice of Snow Lake.

The little one clambered to the spot where the wild blueberries grow.

I didn't know I loved trees, country of trails, switch backs, meadows.

Secondary roads and telling the child—these sticks will soon turn green.

When I see you again it will be when the flashflood river renders talismans from the strewn—I'll stoop, gather the husk, the twig, the feather.

The Blues is the language of catastrophe spoken lyrically.*

*—Cornell West

—*Denise Calvetti Michaels*

Daesh Kills the Bearded Bulls

Here we learned to write
In mud, on stone, here
We learned to write with sticks
In mud baked in the sun for all time
We learned to write in stone with hammers
That now chisel our first words out of time
Crack the mud five thousand years made
This is where we wrote first of the dark
Journey into the deep place tracing
In stone in mud, our wedges prying
Apart the mystery of the mind to count
To read the steps of the journey from the deep
Now that is ripped out of the rock
Torn from the mud, the wedges disappear
Opening the black wound that does not bleed
Burying where we came from in dust
This is Daesh, the end of our beginning
Winged bulls, lion-headed men, here we wrote
Of them, of Astarte first in mud in stone
Here we counted first the sheep, the grain
Here we counted the stars first in mud
Then in stone. Later we turned reeds
Into sheets of time and winged men
And bearded bulls and women in pure white
Now is broken the stone, cracked
The mud—must we dive again
Into that black mystery? Did Muhamad

Know his acolytes would see stone as sin
Mud as crime, and wipe away the wedges
That pried open the pit where light now cannot shine?

—*Jack Remick*

While You Wander

If you keep this poem—this amulet—
inside you, then you will remember

that it is me who will look for your return.
Wherever you go, I will be here

with an open door, the bread rising,
the soup simmering, the apples nearly ripe.

I'll prepare a bed for your weariness,
a lavender bath to soothe your aches.

Beeswax candles will light the way
if moonlight is scarce. If you return

at midday, follow the sun's angle
to the path that leads to my house,

the walk lined with roses, the blue
mailbox announcing your name.

A chorus of crickets will welcome you.
An assembly of finches will sing to you

from the quince. Hummingbirds
will beat their wings eighty times per second

because you have come
back to me, my wanderer, because

the night has been too long
and too dark even though

my eyes stay open and lit
through these hours—

If you wear this amulet
then I will know that you cannot forget

that within its velvet folds
is my solitary wish to keep you

safe from the snake's fang,
the tornado's funnel, the sinking boat

adrift in the absence of current,
all that I cannot keep from you

because you have chosen to step
away, my gypsy, my rambler,

my drifter, in exile from all
that I would make yours,

all that I treasure: you,
and you, and you again.

Here, against my breast,
your beating heart.

—T. Clear

Abide

One day: a clutch of pheasant eggs
at the foot of an apple tree.
The next morning: nothing.
Never mind my frantic pacing
down row after orchard row,
certain I'll stumble upon them
disguised as autumn's crackled leaves.

Where is the hen that yesterday
perched above me in blossoms
just beginning to flare open?
Instead: a dead robin on its back
that I flip with a twig
so that it may face decay
with some small dignity.

Apples too small to be useful
lie puckered at my feet—
I make a heap of the misshapen,
the pocked and cleaved that endured
a winter of snow and perpetual winds.
Here is something imperfect to love,
if not the dead robin or missing eggs.

And here is one half-apple withered
to the shape of an even more imperfect heart—
held to the sun, a fire still burns
at the core. *Let it be enough*
is my insufficient prayer,   *—T. Clear*
and I'll walk away knowing
that it's not.

Ahh, Tootsie, is That You?

Is that you, walking between two fellows
along Poulsbo's main street this morning
between the winter holidays, while I peer
from the window of a strange coffeeshop
between the place I left a while ago and
my next destination?

A tall steeple overlooks murals of vikings,
boating on winter waters across the walls
of bakery buildings, while underdressed
children of Norwegian settlers stroll and
damp cold waits outside, to chill my heart
like you did, remember?

If it's you, please know that I carry no salt
about what you did, having done similarly
when I was young like you still seemed
that afternoon when you sidled up in that
little Skagit county roadhouse and stole
what was left of my affection.

Surprise of surprises, I saved a little bit
hidden away like a Jackson in my shoe, and
searching an old photo you left behind
I discover colonies of your own hard times at
the corner of your mouth, beneath your eyes,
lovers who never returned.

—*Thomas Hubbard*

Homecoming

Cracked mosaic designs,
faded green and brown patterns
glide like wax under mother's
Western State Hospital locked door.

Blue sliver cradles Skagit's*
spawning Chinook. Fingerlings, like dots
and dashes, escape from orange cages,
feast on nutrient rich carcasses
disintegrating in shallows.
Each mouthful ignites prehistoric memories:

>   chasing hordes of silver herring,
>   ravaging clouds of floating krill,
>   and inhaling fluttering ribbons
>   of the Skagit 3,000 miles from home.

Unable to touch my ancestor's ashes
deep in Hiroshima graves, spirits
in red and black tribal robes guide me
like a fingerling to the Salish Sea.

Translucent fishing lines hiss and splay akimbo,
Skagit River bonfires criss-cross rocky shores,
smoldering signal beacon guides me home.

My footsteps are grey shards
in a stream of fractured tiles.
I peer through wire-meshed glass
into mother's empty room.

—Lawrence Matsuda

---
*Skagit River in Washington State

Five Steps—Five By Seven

1. Go game, infinite
possibilities, saucer
shaped black and white stones
arc between thick-arthritic
fingers. Stones snap board.

2. Black sun sculpture hole
frames Space Needle, like strange fruit,
black men hanging from
Magnolias in deep south.

3. Customer mouths agape,
front row Marilyn Monroe
boosts Ella across
music color barrier.

4. King's non-violence
closes color gaps, pockets
and islands remain.
Bullet strikes a hole in hearts.

5. Obama's floppy
disk 2.0 downloads to
American hard
drive. White stone cracks to pieces.

—*Lawrence Matsuda*

Nisei Fall

Fall down seven times, rise up again.
In Rainier's shadow, sacred torii* beckons like Mt. Fuji,
welcome sight after our release from WWII desert prisons.
Cherry blossoms flutter like snow.

—*Lawrence Matsuda*

*_____
Japanese archway gate

Cradle Board

In India, a five day old female infant was left outside the temple by her parents as they already have a five year old girl. They were apprehended just as they tried to tiptoe away from the sleeping infant. The police have placed her in an orphanage till the court decides where the foundling must go, back to parents unwilling to keep her or to the orphanage where she has an equal chance of getting adopted or sold into a sweat shop where her nimble fingers thread sequins into stars.

In USA, "baby boxes," small, opaque, "incubator-like" contraptions are being created so that a person can put a baby inside in order to safely abandon an infant. The boxes, will be placed at spots like police stations, and can only be opened by those who have the key. The pressure of the body being placed in it will also set off an alarm that alerts local emergency medical professionals, so that there is an instant response.

twin jet contrails—
slice through summer clouds
a shrike's staccato cry

—Angelee Deodhar

CHANOYÚ

Rikyu, entre penumbras, vaciado: nadie leguas
    a la redonda, explica el
    Maestro ante la puerta
    de papel de arroz, de
    piernas abiertas explica
    ante las tres sombras
    que se reflejan en la
    puerta corrediza
    (*Seisetsu*, su sombra;
    Joshu, su sombra
    apegada a la sombra
    de *Seisetsu*; y *Kobori*
    Yenshu, su sombra a
    los pies de las sombras
    de *Joshu* y *Seisetsu*)
    que entre los cuatro
    principios que rigen
    la ceremonia del té
    (a rajatabla) (oyeron,
    a rajatabla) un grito
    los acompaña con un
    golpe de vara en el
    hombro izquierdo de
    los tres discípulos en
    la pequeña sala de té
    (golpe que reverbera
    en la penumbra de
    sombra a sombra,
    sólo que en el hombro

derecho se recibe, y
viene a morir al pie
del alarido de *Rikyu*):
a esta hora, en este
día y lugar corresponde
adentrarse (todos) (y
cada uno) en el
concepto (uno de
cuatro) de pureza
que regula, más bien
regimenta, la ceremonia
del té.

Pureza: la ropa recién planchada, ligero olor
a incienso, aroma a
trementina en las
mangas, ropa
reconciliada con
los extremos del
pensamiento, afán
de riqueza (querer
cuatro tarecos
corrientes, de poco
valor material se
considera, entendedlo,
afán de riqueza) afán
de pureza (no hay
mayor peligro, más
sutil extravío, callad,
sombras, callad) toda
obstinación, y entre
todas, la peor

obstrucción consiste
en pensar en la Muerte
(siempre un apego)
creer que se alcanza
la pureza a base de
voluntad y afán.
Creerlo, y en voz
baja, con convicción,
considerarse elemento
puro, ente blanqueado,
viva condición exenta
de máculas, mácula
de las palabras, mácula
de los significados,
pureza de pensamiento,
la alta idea del deber y
claro está, sin necesidad
de afirmarlo, arrogarse
(enderezad el cuerpo)
el derecho a sentarse
al pie del árbol de la
meditación en el
regazo de *Kannon*,
o entre las piernas
fornidas de Buda.

Kobori Yenshu se escabulle y regimenta su
    vida interior con la idea
    de pobreza, *Joshu* se
    contenta con el concepto
    de reverencia, lo pone
    (mental) a prueba

haciendo genuflexiones
(siente a veces la
tentación de hacerle
un corte de manga o
la higa al Maestro)
Seisetsu otorga
primacía a la idea
de tranquilidad, cierra
los ojos, se duerme,
y pese a los varazos
que recibe y reciben
sus sombras, no
despierta. Los tres
saben que *Rikyu* sabe:
juntan sombras, y por
la sombra única de los
tres se escabullen
(mental) a florestas,
campos de amapola,
la orilla de los ríos
cubierta de mantos
de verdolaga, juncias,
menta silvestre, berro,
y se sientan a la sombra
de una sombra, se
ponen a beber té frío
a mansalva, haciendo
gárgaras, ruidos, beben
un té comercial de
exportación, y mezclan
sus clases, verde con
té de Ceilán, té negro

con té de escaramujo
rebajado, y cual si
fueran unos traviesos
novicios abarrotan de
azúcar el fondo de las
tazas (no son siquiera
tazas sino vasos de
cristal corriente): y
tras pelearse por
unos bizcochos
cubiertos, más bien
embarrados por varias
capas de chocolate
industrial, se reportan,
todas sus sombras se
contienen, la sombra
única que los rige se
apacigua al ver a
Rikyu, Maestro de
maestros, en vez de
recriminarlos (reprenderlos)
vituperar sus nombres y
el nombre de todos sus
ancestros (sombras
incluidas) con los
brazos cruzados
sobre la barriga, se
va doblando de risa,
tiembla su cuerpo
al irrumpir en carcajadas,
acaba tirado por los
suelos, por poco

desbarata el *shoji*
de las puertas
corredizas, y los
tres abrazados,
purificados, desprovistos
de nombre, profesión,
adefesio de sombras,
y por encima de todo
para siempre olvidados,
estallan los cuatro entre
risotadas, de espaldas
a *Rikyu*, a fin de cuentas
descartan la equívoca
ceremonia del té.

—José Kozer

Chanoyú

Rikyu, in the dimness, emptied: no one for miles
    around, the
    Master at the rice
    paper door, his
    legs spread wide, explains
    in the midst of three shadows
    reflecting in the sliding door
    (*Seisetsu*, his shadow;
    Joshu, his shadow
    stuck to *Seisetsu's* shadow; and *Kobori*
    Yenshu, his shadow at
    the feet of *Joshu* and *Siesetu's* shadows)
    that among the four principles that determine
    the tea ceremony
    (to the letter of the law) (they heard
    precisely) a scream
    accompanying them with a
    strike from a cane
    on the three disciple's
    left shoulder in
    the small tea room
    (a strike that reverberates
    in the dimness of shadows upon shadows,
    received only on the right shoulder, and
    comes to die at the feet of
    Rikyu's cry):
    this time, corresponding
    to this day and place,
    enters (everyone) (and
    each one) into the

concept (one out of
four) of purity
that regulates, or rather
regiments, the tea
ceremony.

Purity: clothes recently ironed, light fragrance
of incense, aroma of
turpentine on the
sleeves, clothes
reconciled with
opposite thoughts, desire
for richness (longing for
four common utensils, considered
of little material value, understand this,
desire for richness) desire
for purity (there is no
greater danger than
subtle straying, silent,
shadows, silent) any
obstinacy, and in the midst
of everything, the gravest
impediment consists
in thinking about Death
(always affectionate)
believing that one achieves
purity through
will and desire.
Believe it, and in a low
voice, with conviction,
consider pure
elements, whitened entities,

living in a state without
blemish, blotch of words, stain
of meanings,
purity of thought,
the exalted idea of duty and
clearly, there's no need
to affirm, to appropriate,
(straighten your posture)
the right to sit
at the foot of the tree of
meditation at
Kannon's bosom
or at Buddha's
weighty feet.

Kobori Yenshu slips away regimenting his
    interiority with the idea
    of poverty, *Joshu* contents himself
    with the concept of reverence, putting
    (mental) it to the test
    prostrating, genuflecting
    (feeling at times the
    temptation to disregard
    the Master, up yours)
    Seisetsu gives
    supremacy to the idea
    of tranquility, closing
    his eyes, he falls asleep,
    and despite the blows that he
    and his shadows receive,
    he does not awake. All three
    know that *Rikyu* knows:

they gather shadows,
and only through the one shadow
they slip away
(mental) to the glade
to ladybug fields
river's edge
purslane mantels, sedge,
wild mint, watercress
they find a seat alongside the shadow's
shadow, they begin to drink cold tea
copiously, gargling, slurping, drinking
commercially exported tea,
mixing different kinds, green with
Ceylon tea, black tea
diluted Rosehip tea, and as if
they were mischievous novices,
lumping sugar
in the bottom of their
glasses (not even china
only cheap cups):
disputing over tea cakes
covered, or rather
muddied with several
layers of industrial
chocolate, all the shadows
make themselves present
containing, that one shadow that regulates them
calms them seeing
Rikyu, Master among
masters, instead of
reproaching them (rebuking them)
vituperating their names and

the names of all their
ancestors (including
shadows) with arms crossed
at his belly, he doubles
over in laughter,
his body shaking
interrupting guffaws
he ends up on the
ground, barely
missing the *shoji*
of the sliding doors, and the
three embrace,
purified, devoid
of name, profession,
blight of shadow,
and above all, forever forgotten,
they break loose, all four, into
laughter, their backs turned on *Rikyu*,
when it's all over, they
overlook the misguided
tea ceremony.

—*José Kozer*
Translation by Judith K. Lang Hilgartner

CÁNTICO ESPIRITUAL

Donde Dios existe la música existe, sólo la
música lo convoca. Pasión
de San Juan (Bach) (Arvo
Pärt) Dios de atrición la
música lo compunge: lo
lleva a dejarse secar la
frente perlada de sudor,
pedir no lo llamen de
nuevo, con una vez
basta: dejar de saltar
de un ojo a otro astro,
regresar a su escondite,
de espaldas a la
música, Dios vuelve
a la abstracción. Ni
Monte Horeb ni Gólgota,
ni la aparente extensión
del desierto (uno que
otro oasis) ángeles
disfrazados de
camelleros sometidos
de lo alto a la procreación.
La música se deshilvana
en arpegios desmembrados,
notas desmoronadas de
las que cae la nieve (eso
explica lo anterior) llueve
(oíd tabletear el agua
lustral de Dios al

contaminarse en los
techos de hojalata,
abajo): cae la misma
arena de siempre, Dios
la obliga a descender
de las alturas, la música
obliga a Dios: le da la
espalda, quién a quién,
de un manotazo (primero
y último) la convierte en
elementos, estaciones,
desorientaciones, y el
punto cardinal intermedio
y único donde por último
se esconde. Se escondió.
Su silencio, nuestros
coros: su enmudecimiento
nuestros orfeones, todos
visten casulla y bonete,
perderán el hálito y la
voz a la mañana
siguiente. Maraña la
respiración coral que
perderán. Dios no
escucha ya, a la
mañana. Desciende
de su ascenso inicial
una música que se
puso a recontar
Pasión de San
Juan (Bach) (Arvo
Pärt) contar la

irrealidad del Trono,
del Juicio, la Balanza,
los desiertos, toda
lápida en los suelos,
su reguero de ceniza
y de arena, irrealidad.
Copos. Barreduras,
estrías y estribaciones
inasibles. No hay
consecuencias. No
hay efectos: daos
vuelta y veréis que
donde Dios oyó
música (una vez)
no hay causa. Del
número que sigue,
justo para aparentar
continuidad, habrá
floreos, incertidumbres
vocales, oratorios
devaneos del aire,
falaz arquitectura.
Nada es sólido sin
Dios. Nada es sólido
y la voz pesa en
tantos idiomas,
callad. Basta ya,
callad. Y ved cómo
las naves zarparon,
ved cómo Urano y
Gea y sus hijos
sucumbieron. De

incógnita en incógnita
sus armonías entonadas
a sabiendas que no hay
nada, sucumbieron: el
dios que se despeña
lleva cualquier nombre,
indumentaria, un destino
más, dios irrisorio hijo
de Urano (que lo parió)
de Gea (que lo enterró)
dios inhumado. Sustraído
(¿de Dios?). Un dios se
esconde tras otro dios.
¿Desolador? Real.
¿Devastador? Un
punto de aire
(paréntesis) puntos
suspensivos, punto
de música aparte en
el ojo ciclópeo, el ano
de Gea, dídimos de
Urano: y donde Dios
asoma, iba a asomar,
compás final (Bach)
(Arvo Pärt) atriles
para siempre
estropeados,
partituras de muerte
permutadas (no os
sobresaltéis) Dios
dará dos palmadas,
nudo desbaratado,

cantad, cantad la
música para que
Dios acuda se
reanude (nupcial).

—José Kozer
Translator: Judith K. Lang Hilgartner

Spiritual Canticle

Where God exists, music exists, only
    music convokes him. Saint John Passion (Bach) (Arvo
Pärt) God of attrition
music compels him, leads him
to wipe his brow beaded with sweat,
asking that he not be called again,
one time is enough: letting him leap
from an eye to another star,
allowing him to return to his hiding place,
his back turned away from the
music. God returns
to his abstraction. Not
Mount Horeb nor Golgotha,
not the apparent expanse
of the desert (an oasis here
or there) angels
disguised as
subdued camel drivers
from the heights of procreation.
Music unravels
into dismembered arpeggios,
destroyed notes from
falling snow (that
explains what came before) it rains
(listen to God's lustral water pattering
contaminating itself
on tin rooves below): there falls the same
sand as always, God
makes it descend
from the heights, music

compels God: he turns
his back, who to whom,
a slap (the first
and the last) transforms music into
elements, seasons, disorientations, and the
intermediate cardinal point
and in the final coordinate finally
he hides himself. Hid himself.
His silence, our
choirs: his muteness,
our choruses, everyone
dressed in the chausible and birreta,
We will lose our halo and our voices
the next morning. Convoluted breath
will be lost. God is not
listening anymore in the mornings,
Music descends from its initial ascent,
Echoing Saint John's Passion (Bach) (Arvo
Pärt) evoking the unreality of the
Judgment Throne, the Balances, the deserts,
any gravestone on the earth,
Trails of ash and sand, unreality.
Shards. Refuse. intangible grooves
and ditches. There are no consequences.
There are no effects: Turn around and you will see that
from where God heard
music (at one time) there is no reason.
In the song that follows, keeping up the
appearance of continuity, there will be
flourishes, vocal uncertainties,
oratorios flung into the air,
doubtful architecture.

Nothing is solid without
God. Nothing is certain
and voices are weighed down in
so many different languages,
silence. It is enough,
silence. See how
the ships set sail,
see how Uranus and
Gaia and their children
succumbed. From
the unknowable to the mysterious
their well-tuned harmonies
well-knowing that there is
nothing. They succumbed: the
fallen god carries many names
appearances, destinies, one laughable god son
of Uranus (that bore him)
and of Gaia (that buried him)
god laid to rest. Removed
(by God?) A god hides
behind another god.
Distressing? Real.
Devastating? A period.
(parenthesis) Dot, dot,
dot. musical dots,
apart from Cyclops' eye,
Gaia's anus, Uranus' testical:
and where God
appears, was going to appear.
The final measure (Bach)
(Arvo Pärt) music stands
forever broken.
sheet music of death

forever changed. (do not
be frightened) God will clap twice,
the knot unraveled. Sing. Sing music
so that God will listen beginning
again (nuptial).

— JoséKozer
Translation by Judith K. Lang Hilgartner

That Summer

Enticed by the No Swimming sign
we find our own swimming hole,
Tallapoosa Point in Pelham Bay Park.

With my new Brownie I snap photos
ten of us balancing on rocks.
My hair slides down my back to my hips.
Marge and I sport our older sisters'
suits, too big for us to fill.

Billy and Eileen hold hands.
Though he loves her
she loves another and I love him.

We pair off or should I say
we match the boys with the girls
like washed socks.

We are trying to control the thing in us
that was beyond control
like a dog sensing a quake before
it struck. Soon two would slip
among the shadows of the oaks
leave us flat and not look back.

—*Liz Dolan*

After Hiroshima

> *Shikata ga nai*
> August 15, 1945

Each day in school we vow to die for Hirohito,
file past his icon with eyes cast down
as if nine suns might blind us. Even in dreams
his white wings blaze. When we hear his voice
    —an ordinary voice like any other—
    It can't be helped
we are struck dumb except for Akiro who mimics it exactly
    —a twelve year old in tattered shorts
      speaks with the voice of a deity—

—*Liz Dolan*

FRONT LINE MAN
—*for Steve Miller, Vietnam vet*

He's seen too much
he's over-exposed
passed beyond all limits years ago
smashed all the statues he encountered
detonated several hundred minor gods
found the happy medium by accident
and lost it in a bar downtown.

What truths remain intact
which myths still hold their meaning?
Every night another bomb destroys the kitchen
grenades destroy the tunnels in his dreams

Pray for him my friends.
There's no place left for him to run to
They grin behind their triggers
dodge the mines
behind his eyes
and close in
for another
final
kill

—Emmanuel Williams

Untitled Haiku

ciao! little gestalt
pothole — sayonara, wet
Peking duck taco

—Jason Kirk

Untitled Haiku

man with fewer teeth
than the average blowjob
ravages corncob

—*Jason Kirk*

CASTLE ROCK
(Tuba City, Navajo Nation)

It has another name in our language,
though from here, across the airstrip,
I get the idea: red sandstone walls,
corners to shoot arrows from.
I saw ruined castles in Germany,
after my legs, you know, in the Gulf...
Blown apart. Thought they'd stand forever.
In the hospital, I listened
for hours to music—grunge, metal—
until all went missing in the noise.

Now, they're teaching Navajo, here
in the schools, even to Anglos.
My father went to boarding school
off reservation. His father, too.
My grandfather knelt on wood floors
all day—punishment for speaking
what his parents taught him.
His knees bled; they cut his hair.
English stripped his heart naked.
He learned not to talk.

And I...No, wait. Listen... Hear that?
It's the Junior High. They're leading kids
in the pledge: lined up, hearts covered,
like a prayer, the way they taught me.
In the Gulf, I saluted, like Dad in Korea.
Maybe Kit Carson's men did too,
all those years ago, when the Army

drove our people east, away from this,
our land, to make us farmers,
civillized, out of the way.

But we came back—fewer, parts of us
missing. Now there's a reservation,
schools. A council, too: another
Anglo gift. Washington hates
not knowing who's in charge.
One thing's sure: it's never us.
It's good to live in your own country,
but March winds sting with red dust
from land picked clean to heat
other men's homes and make their bombs.

In Flagstaff, I hear them say we get
all we want here on the Rez.
What I got were legs that don't walk
and a goddamn Purple Heart.
If you need heroes, find the Code Talkers.
They've got pictures and ribbons in the
Kayenta Burger King. There, you can lean
near the tables, where tourists talk
over Whoppers and fries,
and read what real men once did.

They were heroes; they are whole.
I'm neither, though what I am
is hard to say—impossible in English.
And even Navajo feels secondhand,
one more sliver of a brokenness
that's said too much already. Leave me,

please, here, alone, the latest ruin
in these crumbling rocks, where I'll listen
for the voice of my grandfather,
who knew when not to speak.

—*Brian Volck*

Dropping the Ball

This field doesn't have any grass. How she
misses the smell of fresh cut grass.
There is no cheering crowd.
Just a bunch of soldiers
playing softball. Before the cotton candy sky
is swallowed up. She waits her turn at bat.
When Sergeant Chaplain walks up to her.
Be at the BDOC Conference room.
Tomorrow. 0430. She starts to speak.
When he says, "I can't tell you anymore."
She goes to the plate. Swings and
not quite gets the meat of the bat on the ball.
So her eye blooms black and blue.
The seam engraved on her cheek bone
as a Lieutenant yells for someone to get some ice.

At 0430, she is told to guard a door
while other soldiers bring in the local interpreters.
This reminds her when she once saw some Indians
netting fish. She is reaching out to her childhood.
Trying to grab onto what is left. --There is a few seconds
where the ball is suspended in the air. When all is quiet
like a mortar right before it hits the ground.
I can tell you. There is no cheering crowd.

—Kristine Iredale

MAIN STREET BANISHMENT

Crash cart nursing corps must
all be Olympic sprinters by now,
though they couldn't save William
Wantling, Andrew Gettler, or all
future-generation others, as I
reread Ed Galing's Army arrival
poem at Dachau, I was reminded
that sometimes service folks need
an ice breaker escort as Operation
Stand Down has offered to assist me
out of this surplus American psyche
sanctioned by others into ascension

—David Pointer

Destierro De Avenida Central

El carro de accidente que cuida el Corp. debe
todos ser esprínteres Olímpicos ya,
aunque ellos no pudieran salvar a Guillermo
Wantling, Andrew Gettler, o todos
otros de futura generación, como mí
la llegada de ejército del Editor releído Galing
poema en Dachau, me recordaron
esto a veces necesidad de gente de servicio
una escolta de rompehielos como Operación
Retírese ha ofrecido asistirme
de esta psique americana de sobra
sancionado por otros en ascensión

—David Pointer

Manila John Basilone

In Marine Corps boot camp
they taught us about Manila
John Basilone, how he was
a hero on Guadalcanal with
two others holding off 3000
Japanese, how on that first
day at Iwo Jima he led the
charge all the way up that
volcanic hill holding a hot
water-cooled 30. caliber
machine gun then John was
topside… blown apart into
ever conspicuous gallantry
posthumously remembered
by all those former young
action type over achievers
who came back home to
negotiate official facades
or false flags or Sunday
dinner with a great family
always thinking of what
others paid to open the
iron gates at Arlington
National Cemetery

—*David S. Pointer*

Manila John Basilone

En Infantería de Marina inicializan campo
ellos nos enseñaron sobre Manila
John Basilone, como él era
un héroe en Guadalcanal con
dos otros que aplazan 3000
Japonés, como en esto primero
día en Iwo Jima él condujo el
cobre en todo esto
colina volcánica que sostiene un caliente
echar agua refrescado 30. calibre
la ametralladora entonces John era
lado superior … hecho volar aparte en
valentía alguna vez visible
póstumamente recordado
por todos aquellos antiguos joven
tipo de acción sobre cumplidores
quién vino en casa a
negocie al funcionario
o banderas falsas o el domingo
comida con una gran familia
siempre pensar que
los otros pagaron a abierto el
puertas de hierro en Arlington
Cementerio Nacional

—*David S, Pointer*

CLINICAL PEARL INCINERATOR

Blocking agent in the community
mental health job interview, this
time: *Marine military police corps
are just like Nazi SS* blurts the
Bachelor level social worker then
negating my ten year journey from
Camelot Housing Project through
Leatherneck land even guarding
President Reagan's travel route
against possible terrorists, and
unknown turmoil after he'd been
shot as I completed graduate work
only to have my grand life joy
backsplashed like tainted plasma

—*David Pointer*

Incinerador De Perla Clínico

El bloqueo de agente en la comunidad
entrevista de trabajo de salud mental, este
tiempo: *Corp. de policía militar marítimo
son justo como SS Nazi* habla sin tino el
Nivel de soltero trabajador social entonces
la negación de viaje de mi diez año de
Plano de Construcción de Camelot por
Tierra de Leatherneck que hasta se protege
La ruta de viajes del presidente Reagan
contra terroristas posibles, y
la confusión desconocida después de que él había sido
tiro cuando completé el trabajo de graduado
sólo tener mi magnífica alegría de vida
backsplashed como plasma corrompido

—David Pointer

Inner Feelings

George wants me to express
inner feelings. I hear
vague voices above or beyond
the radio. The walls talk.
All week I have been with people.
I am glad to be alone now.
Tonight I washed hair in the shower,
pulled on sweats, cuddly cottons.
Tossed salad with avocado,
tomato and artichoke hearts
for dinner. Now I sip decaffeinated
Irish cream. My coffee carafe
did not crack this morning
the way my thoughts did. Water
pearls on the ceiling
of the shower. I patted bath powder
on my chest and back, a puff
under the elastic of my underwear,
belly and rear. I am clean; my hair dries
in the air. The same Vance Hotel
sign that I saw out the barred window
of the institution shines red
where I now live.
I am lonely for myself. I will read
a story aloud. My voice will break
the silence.

—Crysta E. Casey

The Boat

Kim came over the night
I found out I had a shadow
on my stomach.
She was a cross-dresser—
a bomber pilot in Vietnam,
now in my Women's
Straight and Sober Group.
We drank wine that night.
She told me she had been
the son of the president of Chrysler
in Detroit, and when
the song played, "I was not
the chosen one . . ." she said,
"I was the chosen one."

Kim lived at the Morrison Hotel,
a rundown, rat-and-roach infested
example of public housing in Seattle,
across from the Court House.
She lay in bed and watched TV
most of the time. Once she brought
a noose to the group, said she wanted
to go on the long sleep. That night
we talked, she said, "You don't have
stomach cancer."

I wanted to paint
a boat down by the water.
It was in a state of decay
but I wanted to capture the beauty of its shadow

on the water—like an x-ray.
I needed to look at the boat in detail,
the cabin doors, the life boat,
the flags flying.

Kim gave me her paints.
They did an M.R.I., shot me
with intravenous iodine. Still something there,
so they sent a camera down my stomach,
said it was fine.
Kim called to go out to Ivar's.
She would treat me. My answering machine
took the message. I never got back
to her. She hung herself on a Friday.
Two weeks later, I went down to paint the boat.
It was gone.

—Crysta E. Casey

MIRACLE

Last night I performed
a miracle. I poured
the bottle I had left
down the drain. I turned wine
into water.

—Crysta E. Casey

V.A. Smoke Shack

In a loosely-tied robe, the man with stump legs,
in a wheelchair, his gray hair pulled back
in a ponytail, swaps tales with another vet,
peanut butter in C-rats and M-16s
that clogged in the mud. One old man says,
"I don't know nothin 'bout Vietnam."
He's from WWII, lost on a long shot,
still betting the Kentucky Derby
that afternoon on TV. The nurse
on the night shift tells me about neighbors
who make too much noise getting drunk,
letting their kid jump on the floor.
"Shoulda never bought that place
near the airport. When planes take off
going north, the house rattles
and I wear earplugs."
The vets in the smoke shack
stare at the sky with lost eyes
when a plane flies over. A man says,
"They're going to remove half my face.
It was always my bad side." Another says
he has a cowboy hat like that other vet
from Idaho, but he doesn't wear it.
"I think I'm being punished," says the old
man who asks for a light.

—Crysta E. Casey

Biographies

Charles O'Hay— Since 1987, my work has appeared in over 125 literary publications including *The New York Quarterly, Cortland Review, Gargoyle, West Branch,* and *Mudfish*. In 1995, I received a Pennsylvania Council on the Arts fellowship in poetry. My two collections of poems—*Far from Luck* (2011) and *Smoking in Elevators* (2014)—were published by Lucky Bat Books.

Tess Gallagher— Her ninth volume of poetry, is *Midnight Lantern: New and Selected Poems,* from Graywolf Press and Bloodaxe Press in England. Forthcoming in April is *Boogie-Woogie Crisscross,* a collaboration with Lawrence Matsuda from MadHat Press. Other poetry includes *Dear Ghosts, Moon Crossing Bridge,* and *Amplitude*. Her *A Path to the Sea,* translations of Liliana Ursu's by Adam Sorkin, Ms. Gallagher and Ms. Ursu came out in 2011. Gallagher's *The Man from Kenvara: Selected Stories* was published fall 2009. *Barnacle Soup—Stories from the West of Ireland,* a collaboration with the Sligo storyteller Josie Gray, is available in the US from Carnegie Mellon. *Distant Rain,* a conversation with the highly respected Buddhist nun, Jacucho Setouchi, of Kyoto, is both an art book and a cross-cultural moment. Gallagher is also the author of Soul Barnacles: *Ten More Years with Ray; A Concert of Tenses: Essays on Poetry,* and two collections of short fiction: At the *Owl Woman Saloon* and *The Lover of Horses and Other Stories*. She spearheaded the publication of Raymond Carver's *Beginners* in Library of America's complete collection of his stories published Fall 2009 and is forthcoming as a stand alone volume in 2015. Most recently she shepherded the use of Raymond Carver's poem and story in the film *Birdman,* directed by Alejandro Inarritu. She spends time in a cottage on Lough Arrow in Co. Sligo in the West of Ireland where many of her new poems are set, and also lives and writes in her hometown of Port Angeles, Washington.

Jerome Gold PhD—is the author of fifteen books, including *The Moral Life of Soldiers and the memoir, Paranoia & Heartbreak: Fifteen Years in a Juvenile Facility*. Russell Banks said about this book: "I've finished reading Jerome Gold's terrific book cover to cover without a break… It's a powerful and very tenderhearted book without a soupçon of sentimentality. Unforgettable!" Mr. Gold's novels include *Sergeant Dickinson*, about which the *New York Times Book Review* said: "[It] belongs on the high, narrow shelf of first-rate fiction about battlefield experience." He has published stories, essays, reviews and poems in *Chiron Review, Moon City Review, Fiction Review, Boston Review, Hawaii Review*, and other journals.

Doug Johnson PhD—The founding editor of Cave Moon Press, he has published in numerous literary journals with his artwork and poetry. His collection of short stories, *Frank's Diary* was nominated for the Pacific Northwest Bookseller's Award in 2009. His debut novel *The GΦlden Years: The First Half* published by Bennett and Hastings in 2013. He works in multiple disciplines. He gained a 'Thank You' note from President Obama for his symphonic prelude composed in his honor. His visual art appears in *In the shadow of a master: The artwork of Alfredo Arreguin and Doug Johnson*. This collaborative art exhibit with Alfredo Arreguin appears in the Yakima Valley Museum in 2016. Collaborate at cavemoonpress@gmail.com.

Kathleen Flenniken—began her career as a civil engineer and didn't discover poetry until her early 30s. Her collection, *Plume* (University of Washington Press, 2012) , a meditation on the Hanford Nuclear Site and her home town of Richland, Washington, won the Washington State Book Award and was a finalist for the William Carlos Williams Award from the Poetry Society of America and the Pacific Northwest Book Awards. Her first book, Famous (University of Nebraska Press, 2006), won the Prairie Schooner Book Prize in

Poetry and was named a Notable Book by the American Library Association . Her other honors include a Pushcart Prize and fellowships from the National Endowment for the Arts and Artist Trust. She was the 2012 – 2014 Washington State Poet Laureate.

Gerry MacFarland—is a co-editor at *Floating Bridge Press* in Seattle. His work has appeared in *Crab Creek Review, Crucible, Limestone, Meridian Anthology of Contemporary Poetry, Sanscrit, Zyzzyva, Contemporary American Voices*, and many others. He has been a finalist in the Grayson Books chapbook contest, *December's* poetry contest, The Frost Place competition, and won 2nd Place in the 2015 Gemini contest. In 2016, his poetry will appear in *Cider Press Review, Chautauqua, and Salt Hill Journal*.

Charles Potts—Recent books include *Pilgrim* and *Martel* from Least Bittern Books, *The Source* and a reprint of *Valga Krusa* in two volumes, *The Yellow Christ* and *Laffing Water* from Green Panda Press; *The Portable Potts* and *Inside Idaho* from West End Press; *Kiot: Selected Early Poems 1963-1977, Lost River Mountain, & Slash and Burn* with Robert McNealy from Blue Begonia Press; a reprint of *Little Lord Shiva: The Berkeley Poems*, 1968, from Glass Eye Books; *Nature Lovers* from Pleasure Boat Studio; and *Across the North Pacific* from Slough Press in College Station, Texas. Potts has been publishing since 1963.

In addition to Potts' work as a poet, he is a publisher of books by thirty other poets thru Tsunami Inc. and Litmus Inc., the editor/publisher of *Litmus* and *The Temple* magazines. He recently donated his literary archive to the Merrill-Cazier Library at Utah State University in Logan, Utah, where he frequently goes to teach and read.

Some people find it helpful to know that in May of 1991 in Winter Park, Colorado, Charles Potts was certified as a Master Practitioner in the Society of Neuro-Linguistic Programming by Steven and Connierae Andreas of NLP Comprehensive. It has been certified in other words that he has mastered the societal practice of talking about his program until he gets on your nerves.

Michael Daley— Michael Daley's poems have appeared recently in *Rhino, Gargoyle, North American Review, Raven Chronicles,* and elsewhere. Pleasure Boat Studio published his translation of *Alter Mundus* by Italian poet Lucia Gazzino, and *Of a Feather* was recently published by Empty Bowl, a division of Pleasure Boat Studio

Amalio Madueño— lives in the Upper Rio Grande region of New Mexico. Poetry prizes include: Pequod Prize (USD-1974); Chicano Literary Prize of Southern California (1975); Wyoming Review Poetry Prize (1979). Recent periodicals featuring his work include *MalPais Review* (2015 Placitas, NM); *Pedestal(2011), China Poetry Review* (Hong Kong, 2013), *Qinghai Poetry Festival Anthology* (Beijing 2012), *PageBoy* (Seattle);*Venus in the Badlands* (Santa Fe); *Between Sleeps: The 315 Project* (Dinsmore & Alley, Vancouver 2006), *Wandering Hermit Review* (Seattle, 2006), *Muse6* (El Paso, 2006) *Sin Fronteras* (El Paso, 2005) , *Border Senses* (El Paso, 2009-2012) *MasTequila* (ABQ, NM), *Askew* (Ventura, CA) and *Earthships: New MexicoPoetry Tangents Anthology* (2007). His latest of 18 chapbooks include *Migra Letters* (2015), *Petroglyph* (2015), *Amexica* (2010), and *Leap Year* (2012). Feature length books include: *Lost In The Chamiso* (Wild Embers Press, 2006 Ashland, OR.), *Cuyamungué* and *Spider Road* (MouthFeel Press, El Paso, 2012). He is currently completing a translation of 10 new poems by 2013 Pablo Neruda Prize winner José Kozer.
The *Border Poetics Consortium*, of which he is principal, consults on poetry program development, events, organizational management and

fundraising. His clients have included Washington Poetry Association (Seattle), Burning Word Poetry Festival (Whidbey Island) Poets Against War (Port Townsend, WA), Beyond Baroque Literary Arts Council (Los Angeles), Hollywood Institute of Poetics (Los Angeles) the Border Book Festival (Las Cruces, NM). He assisted the Spoken Word Lab of Seattle (SPLAB) on the planning, design and development of the 2013, 2014 and 2015 *Cascadia Poetry Festivals.*

Jenifer Browne Lawrence—is the author of *One Hundred Steps from Shore* (Blue Begonia, 2006). Awards include the Orlando Poetry Prize, the James Hearst Poetry Prize, Potomac Review's Poetry Award, and a Washington State Artist Trust GAP grant. Recent work appears or is forthcoming in *Bellevue Literary Review, Los Angeles Review, Narrative, North American Review, Rattle,* and elsewhere. She is co-editor of the Seattle-based literary journal, *Crab Creek Review.* Her second full length book won the Perugia Press contest with *Grayling* and was released in 2015. Born in Oakland, California in 1958, Lawrence was raised in Alaska, and educated at Washington State University. She lives in Poulsbo, a small seaside community west of Seattle.

Sam Hamill—is the author of 16 volumes of poetry, 4 volumes of prose on poetry, and more than two dozen volumes translated from ancient Chinese, Japanese, Greek, Latin, and Estonian. His *Habitation: Collected Poems* was recently published by Lost Horse Press. He lives in Anacortes, Washington, with his bodhisattva, a miniature Australian shepherd, Tara.

Paul Nelson—is a poet, interviewer, essayist. He founded Seattle Poetics LAB & the Cascadia Poetry Festival & wrote *American Sentences* (poetry, 2015), *A Time Before Slaughter* (poetry, shortlisted for a 2010 Genius Award by The Stranger) *Organic Poetry* (essays) and *Organic in Cascadia: A Sequence of Energies* (book-length-essay, Lumme Editions, Brazil, 2013).

He's interviewed Allen Ginsberg, Michael McClure, Sam Hamill, José Kozer, Robin Blaser, Nate Mackey, Joanne Kyger, George Bowering, Brenda Hillman and Daphne Marlatt, presented poetry/poetics in London, Brussels, Nanaimo, Qinghai & Beijing, China, has had work translated into Spanish, Chinese & Portuguese & writes an American Sentence every day.

Awarded a residency at The Lake, from the Morris Graves Foundation in Loleta, CA, he's published work in Golden Handcuffs Review, Zen Monster, Hambone, and elsewhere. Winner of the 2014 Robin Blaser Award from The Capilano Review, he lives in the Duwamish River watershed.

Denise Calvetti Michaels—*Paterson Literary Review, City Works Press, Yours Truly, Crosscurrents* and other journals and anthologies including The Milk of Almonds, *Feminist Press*; Beyond Forgetting, *Kent State University Press*; In Praise of Farmlands, *Whit Press* and between sleeps, *en theos press*; and the 2012 Redmond Centennial Poetry Project. In 2008 she was awarded the Crosscurrents Prize for her prose poem, "Notes from New Orleans" by the Washington Community College Humanities Association. A 2010 fellow of the Jack Straw Writers Program and graduate of Artist Trust EDGE Professional Development Program for Writers, she works as Associate Faculty of Psychology at Cascadia Community College in Bothell, Washington. Her collection *Rustling Wrens* (Cave Moon Press, 2012) won a 4Culture grant to help at-risk families. She is pursuing the MFA in Creative Writing and Poetics from UW Bothell. She lives in Kirkland with her husband, Kirk, near their children and grandchildren. More information is available at: www.rustlingwrens.blogspot.com

Jack Remick—is a novelist and poet. He is the author of *Blood, Gabriela and The Widow*, the poetry collection, *Satori* as well as *The California Quartet: The Deification, Valley Boy, The Book of Changes, and Trio*

of Lost Souls. Gabriela and The Widow was a finalist for the Montaigne Medal and the ForeWord Magazine Book of the Year Award. He and Bob Ray co-authored *The Weekend Novelist Writes a Mystery.* Remick is active in the Seattle writing community. He maintains a blog: http://jackremick.com

T. Clear—a Seattle native, is a founder of *Floating Bridge Press* and Easy Speak open mic series. She has been writing and publishing for nearly forty years; her work has appeared in many journals and magazines including *Poetry Northwest, Cascadia Review, Fine Madness, Poetry Atlanta, Cirque Journal, Seattle Review* and *The Moth.*

Thomas Hubbard— Since retirement from teaching in the Tulalip Heritage School, he has published several authors under his Gazoobi Tales imprint. He writes and edits for *Raven Chronicles* and *Cartier Street Review* magazines, and has featured in many Pacific Northwest spoken word venues. His poems and short stories have appeared in *Yellow Medicine Review, Red Ink, Cartier Street Review, Section 8 Magazine, Raven Chronicles, Florida Review,* and others. He reviews books for various publications, and is available for freelance editing, layout, graphics and book design. His ancestors are Miami, Cherokee, Irish and English and probably others.

Lawrence Matsuda PhD— was born in the Minidoka, Idaho Concentration Camp during World War II. He and his family were among the approximately 120,000 Japanese Americans and Japanese held without due process for approximately three years or more. Currently he is a career educator/writer.

In 2005, he and two Seattle University colleagues co-edited the book, *Community and difference: teaching, pluralism and social justice,* Peter Lang Publishing, New York. It won the 2006 National Association of Multicultural Education Phillip Chinn Book Award. In July of 2010, his book of poetry entitled, *A Cold Wind from Idaho* was published by Black Lawrence Press in New York. His poems appear in *Ambush Review, Raven Chronicles, New Orleans Review, Floating Bridge Review, Black Lawrence Press website, Poets Against the War website, Cerise Press, Nostalgia Magazine, Plumepoetry, Malpais Review, Zero Ducats, Surviving Minidoka* (book), *Meet Me at Higos* (book), *Minidoka-An American Concentration Camp* (book and photographs), Tidepools Magazine, and the Seattle Journal for Social Justice. His second book of poetry, *Glimpses of a Forever Foreigner*, was released in August of 2014. It is collaboration between Matsuda and artist Roger Shimomura who contributed 17 original sketches. In 2015, Matsuda collaborated with artist, Matt Sasaki, and produced two graphic novels: *An American Hero -Shiro Kashino and Fighting for America: Nisei Soldiers* available through the Nisei Veterans Committee Foundation or the Wing Luke Museum.

Dr. Ms. Angelee Deodhar— is an eye surgeon by profession as well as a haiku poet, translator, and artist. She lives and works in India. Her haiku, haibun and haiga have been published internationally in various books and journals, and her work can be viewed on many websites. She does not maintain her own website.

To promote haiku in India, she has translated six books of haiku from English to Hindi. These include: *If Someone Asks: Masaoka Shiki's Life and Haiku* (2005), *Haiku: A Master's Selection*, edited by Miura Yuzuru (2006), *Ogura Hyakunin Isshu: 100 Poems by 100 Poets*(2007), *Children's Haiku from Around the World–A Haiku Primer* (2007), *Indian Haiku* (2008), and *The Distant Mountain: The Life and Haiku of Kobayashi Issa* (2009).

In 2014 and in 2015 she edited two haibun anthologies *Journeys* and *Journeys 2015* which together feature 271 haibun by 56 writers from around the world.

José Kozer PhD—was born in Havana, Cuba (1940) of Jewish parents who emigrated from Poland (father) and Czechoslovakia (mother); he left his native land in 1960, lived in New York until 1997, the year in which he retired from Queens College as Full Professor, where he taught Spanish and Latin American literatures for thirty-two years. After living for two years in Torrox (Málaga), Spain, he moved twelve years ago to Hallandale, Florida, USA. Kozer graduated with a BA from New York University in 1965, and received his MA and PhD from Queens College, CUNY in 1970 and 1983 respectively. He was the recipient of the Premio de Poesía Iberoamericana Pablo Neruda (Chile) for 2013. He is the author of 63 poetry collections, as of early 2014.

His poetry has been partially translated to English, Portuguese, German, French, Italian, Hebrew and Greek, has been widely anthologised and has appeared in numerous literary journals from all over the world. There are several master and doctoral dissertations written on his work, as well as full chapters written (and being written) in several MA and PhD dissertations. His work has been studied in many graduate and undergraduate courses. On José Kozer's poetry there was a Symposium held in 1997 at UCLA (Irvine) which was organized by Prof. Jacobo Sefamí, out of which a full length book was published by UNAM University in Mexico City under the title *La voracidad grafómana: José Kozer*.

Judith K. Lang Hilgartner—is a PhD student and and a Rachel Winer Manin Jewish Studies Fellow from the University of Virginia. She specializes in Contemporary Latin American Jewish Studies as well as Sephardic Studies. She is particularly interested in issues of exile and trauma in post-Holocaust poetry. Her affinity for translation began during her childhood, a skill she learned to employ with friends from the Dominican Republic. It was there that she learned to dance to the rhythm of merengue and to make fried plantains. In her free time, Judith enjoys cooking, playing piano, and reading dictionaries.

Liz Dolan— Her first poetry collection, *They Abide*, was nominated for The Robert McGovern Prize, Ashland University. Her second, *A Secret of Long Life*, nominated for a Pushcart, has been published by Cave Moon Press. An eight-time Pushcart nominee and winner of Best of the Web, she was a finalist for Best of the Net 2014. She won The Nassau Prize for nonfiction and fiction.

Emmanuel Williams— Years ago I knew a Vietnam vet–Steve Miller. Stumpy little guy. Tunnel rat. Told me he crawled along the tunnels Vietnamese villagers dug to escape from the war. He said he dragged kids out and pregnant women and watched them get shot. When I wrote Front Line Man I read it to him in his kitchen where he was sitting with a couple of vet buddies sharing a joint. When I finished he was curled up on the floor, whimpering.
He said, "How did you know?"
I said, "Because you told me."
Steve's dead now. Agent Orange zapped his liver.
Last year Michael Kimpbell, a Bay Area composer, wrote music for Front Line Man and two more war poems, and I read it in St Mark's Church with the San Francisco Sinfonietta. As I read it I was praying that by now Steve was at peace, far from this domain where we do such terrible things to one another

Jason Kirk— is the author of *A Fabulous Hag in Purple on the Moor*, *The Other Whites in South Africa*, and *Reverb*, as well as the composer of "The Mirror of Simple Souls," an opera collaboration with librettist and poet Anne Carson. His most recent publication is a narrative poem ("The Guardian from the Sea") about a wheelchair-bound mermaid who works in an adult-video store in Southern California, which appears in the story anthology *Phantasma*. He lives in Seattle.

Brian Volck— is a pediatrician who received his MFA in creative writing from Seattle Pacific University. His first collection of poetry, *Flesh Becomes Word*, was released by Dos Madres Press in October, 2013. His memoir, *Attending Others: A Doctor's Education in Bodies and Words*, was published by Cascade in August, 2016.

Kristine Iredale— Kristine Iredale is currently a student at Eastern Washington University. In 2008, she deployed with the Washington State Army National Guard's 81st Brigade Heavy Combat Team in Operation Iraqi Freedom. Her poems have appeared in O-Dark-Thirty, RiverLit, The Railtown Almanac, and Northwest Boulevard.

David Pointer—was the son of a piano playing bank robber who died when David was 3 years old. David's grandmother socialized him to be an American service man. Later David served in the United States Marine Corps military police. Today, he serves on the advisory panel at Writing for Peace. His most recent book is entitled *Beyond Shark Tag Bay* online at Blurb Books, and his most recent poetry chapbook is *Bookmobile* at Crisis Chronicles Press.

Crysta E. Casey— (1952-2008) was born in Pasadena, California. She graduated from The State University of New York, Stony Brook, in 1976, where she was one of the founding members of The Women Writers Workshop. After college, she became the first woman hired by the City of Irvine, California, in Parks and Maintenance. In 1978, she enlisted in the all-new voluntary military, serving in the U.S. Marine Corps as a journalist, then as a self-declared "Resident Poet" until her honorable discharge under medical conditions in 1980. She moved to Seattle, Washington in the early 1980s, where she studied with the poet Nelson Bentley and collaborated with Esther Altshul Helfgott on the It's About Time Writers Reading Series. Her first collection of poetry, *Heart Clinic*, was published in 1993 (Bellowing Ark Press). In 2004 she received a Hugo House Award from Richard

Hugo House, and, in 2006, she was a finalist for Seattle Poet Populist. In 2010, Floating Bridge Press brought out a chapbook of her work, *Green Cammie*. *Rules for Walking Out* was the last manuscript Crysta completed and approved before her death at the Seattle VA in the spring of 2008. It was published by Cave Moon Press in June 2016. Crysta's papers are housed in the University of Washington Libraries, Special Collections.

www.ingramcontent.com/pod-product-compliance
Lightning Source LLC
Chambersburg PA
CBHW060202050426
42446CB00013B/2960